Copyright ©2021
All rights Reserved
ILLUSTRATOR: Aneeza Ashraf
Graphic Design Consultant Kevin Dalton
Kevin Dalton Design - kmdaltonxps@gmail.com

this book belongs to

_____

Dedication

This book is dedicated in memory of my parents, Audrey, and Harold Farrar Sr.

I love to see the sun in the morning, it is bright and has a circular shape.

Me encanta ver el sol en la mañana brillante y en un círculo O.

What a pretty ring so clear and shaped in a diamond <> or rhombus.

Qué anillo tan bonito tan claro y en forma en un diamante <> o rombo.

This book I am reading is interesting and in a square shape.

Este libro que estoy leyendo es interesante y en forma cuadrada.

I can squeeze a balloon and it will appear like an oval shape.

Puedo apretar un globo para que tenga una forma ovalada.

Here is an interesting shape, a Parallelogram.

Aquí hay una forma interesante un Paralleograma.

Let's not forget the shape of stars at night, also some snowflakes are also shaped like stars.

No olvidemos la forma de la estrella por la noche y también algunos copos de nieve tienen forma de estrellas.

For Valentines we have many heart shapes.

Para San Valentín tenemos muchas formas de corazón.

The Moon has another appearance, it has a crescent shape at night.
La Luna tiene otra apariencia de Media Luna en forma por la noche.

Grandmas delicious pie is sliced in a pie shape.

El delicioso pastel de las abuelas se corta en forma de pastel.

I see a big cross on top of the hill side.

Veo una cruz gran en la cima de la colina.

About the Author

Gale Dalton IS THE MOTHER OF SEVEN CHILDREN (SIX BOYS AND ONE GIRL) AND HAS 13 GRANDCHILDREN. She established two mentoring groups, Daughters of Destiny for young ladies and Brothers with a Purpose for young men.

Fun with Shapes is her third book. The first book is Beams from Heaven, a poetry compilation, and her second book is Fun with Colors in Espanol y Ingles. Learn more about Author Gale Dalton at

www.galedalton.com

www.ingramcontent.com/pod-product-compliance
Lightning Source LLC
Chambersburg PA
CBHW060306010526
44108CB00041B/2589